Contents

The English alphabet

The English alphabet is listed below.

Capital letters:

A B C D E F G H I J K L M N O P Q R S T U V W X Y Z

Lower case letters:

a b c d e f g h i j k l m n o p q r s t u v w x y z

Note: The letter 'a' can also be written 'a', and the letter 'g' can also be written 'g'.

A sentence begins with a capital letter and ends with a full stop.

There are some letters we call **vowels**. These letters are:

a e i o u

Sometimes 'y' acts as a vowel. This occurs when 'y' has the sound of 'i' in any word.

For example:

by my sky fly try cry

All other letters in the alphabet are called **consonants**. These letters are:

b c d f g h j k l m n p q r s t v w x y z

Articles

The words 'a', 'an' and 'the' are called **articles**: 'a' and 'an' are called **indefinite articles**, and 'the' is called the **definite article**.

Indefinite articles

The words 'a' and 'an' are called **indefinite articles**. They are used:

- to introduce a noun (see chapter on **Nouns**) for the first time.

> He gave me **a** book.

'a' is the indefinite article; it introduces the noun 'book'.

- when there is more than one of the noun and it does not matter which one we are talking about.

> Please open **a** window.

There are many different windows. It does not matter which one you open. Open any window.

'a' is used if the following word begins with a consonant sound; 'an' is used if the following word begins with a vowel sound.

For example, the following sentences are wrong:

*I ate **a** egg. I will wait **a** hour.*

They should be:

*I ate **an** egg. I will wait **an** hour.*

This is because the words 'egg' and 'hour' begin with a vowel sound.

Use **a/an** with a singular noun.

*I bought **a** tomato.*

Use **some** with a plural noun.

*I bought **some** tomatoes.*

a)   I ate _____ apple.

b)   I would like _____ book.

c)   I need _____ hat.

d)   I ate _____ orange for lunch.

e)   He studied for _____ exam.

Definite articles

The word 'the' is called the **definite article**. This is used:

• the second time we talk about a noun. The noun has already been introduced to us.

> He gave me **a** book. (first time)
> I liked **the** book he gave me. (second time)

• when there is only one of the noun.

> **The** sun is shining.
> **The** earth is round.

Use 'the' with both singular and plural nouns.

*Alan ate **the** tomato.*

*Alan ate **the** tomatoes.*

2 Complete each sentence with 'a', 'an' or 'the'.

a)   I want _____ ice-cream.

b)   Do you have _____ pen?

c)   _____ moon is bright tonight.

d) I saw _____ dog outside. Sally was talking to _____ dog.

e) I brought _____ umbrella with me. I hope I won't need to use _____ umbrella.

f) I live next to _____ school. _____ school is new.

g) She bought _____ television yesterday.

h) This is _____ picture. Did you draw it?

i) I saw _____ movie yesterday. It was funny.

j) I can see _____ black cat in _____ garden. Is it yours?

3 Complete each sentence with 'some' or 'the'.

a) There are _____ ants in our kitchen.

b) I will buy _____ grapes for lunch.

c) There are _____ flowers in my garden.

d) Yesterday I gave _____ oranges to Jane. She said _____ oranges were delicious.

e) I put _____ needles in my sewing box. _____ needles were sharp.

f) The teacher gave _____ books to the students today.

g) I bought two tables yesterday. _____ tables are green.

h) Marie has three children. _____ children are lovely.

i) I bought _____ apples for dessert. _____ apples are fresh.

j) I have two dogs. _____ dogs are best friends.

Determiners

Determiners are words that are used for asking, pointing out or showing that someone owns something (possession).

Examples

Determiners when asking something:

which	**Which** painting is famous?
whose	**Whose** car is that?
what	**What** is your friend like?

Determiners when pointing something out:

a	There is **a** problem with the computer.
an	There was **an** elephant on the road.
the	**The** boy is very excited.
that	**That** restaurant is excellent.
these	**These** noodles are very good.
those	**Those** books are old.

Determiners when looking at possession (who owns something):

my, mine	**My** mother is happy.
our, ours	**Our** house is small.
your, yours	**Your** jacket is brown.
her, hers, his	It is **her** book.
its, their	He borrowed **their** tools.

My first day in a new country.

a) I picked up _____ bag from the airport.

    i) my   ii) mine   iii) ours

b) We did not know _____ taxi to choose.

    i) which   ii) these   iii) the

c) The driver took us to _____ hotel.

    i) those   ii) our   iii) what

d) The next day, we caught _____ bus into the city.

    i) those   ii) that   iii) a

e) We enrolled in _____ English school.

    i) a   ii) an   iii) which

f) The teacher asked, '_____ class would you like?'

    i) Which   ii) Those   iii) That

g) '_____ students look friendly,' I said.

    i) Whose   ii) That   iii) Those

h) We went to visit _____ sister.

    i) its   ii) my   iii) that

i) We knocked on _____ door.

    i) her   ii) a   iii) what

j) 'Hello,' she said. 'Welcome to _____ new home!'

    i) his   ii) their   iii) your

Nouns

A **noun** names a person, an animal, an idea or a thing. It is sometimes called a 'naming word'.

These words are all nouns:

| dog | woman | computer | school |

Does it tell me the name of something?

To test if a word is a noun, ask yourself these questions:

- Does it tell me something's name?

| above | | ✗ |
| bed | | ✔ |

- Can I put a determiner such as 'the', 'a' or 'an' in front of it?

| the tree | | ✔ |
| the speak | | ✗ |

If you answer yes to one or both questions, then the word is a noun.

Try testing these words to see if they are nouns:

| cup happy finger hot flower grass has always sock |

1 Put a tick (✔) in the box if the word is a noun; put a cross (✗) if it is not a noun.

beautiful ☐	dog ☐	and ☐	exciting ☐
box ☐	book ☐	when ☐	next ☐
table ☐	slowly ☐	is ☐	girl ☐

8

Proper nouns

These nouns are the names of people, places, organisations, special events, etc. **Proper nouns** always start with a capital letter.

Example:

Rebecca travelled to **America**.

My name is Bill.

The words 'Rebecca' and 'America' are both proper nouns.

You usually do not put 'the' or 'a' with proper nouns.

These words are also proper nouns:

Christmas Day, Paris, Karen, New Zealand, Korea, Hong Kong

Now write down some proper nouns you know:

_____

_____

_____

2 Circle the nouns in the sentences below.

a) Boris the cat ran across the road.

My name is Alice.

b) Sue was wearing a dress.

c) Tom had a dog, a cat, a rabbit and a bird.

d) Mary bought a car.

e) The man had a bed, a table and a chair.

3 Now underline the nouns.

a)   My wife drove to the beach.

b)   We put an umbrella in the sand.

c)   Craig and Lara opened the basket.

d)   Lara rubbed sunscreen on the baby.

e)   The water was very warm.

f)   Craig played in the waves.

g)   Tameka built a sandcastle.

h)   Kevin swam out to a boat.

i)   We ate the sandwiches.

j)   We walked around the rocks and saw a fish.

Brainstorm: Look around you. Write down all the nouns you can see (for example, table, chair, student, teacher, book).

_____

_____

_____

_____

4 Now choose the noun that best fits each sentence.

a)   She stood up and turned off the _____.

    i)   TV   ii)   dog   iii)   book

b)   The dog barked at the _____.

    i)   flower   ii)   stranger   iii)   bread

c)   The bus drove down the _____.

    i)   house   ii)   road   iii)   carpark

d) Ben drove his _____ very quickly.

   i) ball   ii) potato   iii) car

e) The cat ate the _____ .

   i) shoe   ii) paper   iii) meat

5 Decide which word is a proper noun and then rewrite it correctly on the line below.

a)   table   chair   neil

   _____

b)   sunday   box   flower

   _____

c)   buy   telephone   england

   _____

d)   angel   christmas   tree

   _____

e)   paula   rain   library

   _____

f)   shell   pot   easter

   _____

g)   rome   cushion   book

   _____

h)   jar   shoe   spain

   _____

i)   hair   television   mr mills

   _____

j)   snow   moscow   school

   _____

6 Complete the sentences using the proper nouns in the box below.

Miss Smith   Friday   John   Nile   Egypt   London   England
Monday   November

'Well, it is finally a) _____ ,' said b) _____ to

the students. 'Today we are going to have a short test. Who can tell me

the name of the famous river in c) _____ ?'

d) _____ put up his hand. 'The e) _____ ,' he

answered.

'Well done!' answered the teacher. 'Now, what is the capital city of

f) _____ ?'

'g) _____ !' called out another student.

'Great,' said the teacher. 'Now, who can tell me how many days there

are in h) _____ ?'

'Thirty,' answered Sharon.

'Correct!' Miss Smith smiled. 'Okay, time to go. Have a good weekend,

and I'll see you all on i) _____ .'

7 Now make matching pairs.

For example:

A person ————————————→ Elvis Presley

A country	December
A month	Michael Jordan
A person	London
A day	Russia
A city	Wednesday

Singular nouns and plural nouns

Nouns can be either **singular** (about one single person or thing):

girl book apple

or **plural** (about two or more people or things):

girls books apples

Plural nouns

Most plural nouns are formed by adding 's' to the singular noun, for example the plural of 'dog' is 'dogs' (one dog, two dogs). Some plural nouns, however, are formed differently.

Singular noun ending in 'y'

If the noun ends in 'y':

- and there is a vowel before the 'y', add 's' to form the plural, for example key, keys.

- and there is a consonant before the 'y', change the 'y' to 'i' and add 'es' to form the plural, for example family, families.

8 Write the plural of the word in brackets.

a)   The _____ buzzed around the barbecue. (fly)

b)   Karen ate all the _____ off the cake. (cherry)

c)   The _____ screamed loudly. (baby)

d)   We bought two _____ for our Christmas dinner. (turkey)

e)   I have read many _____ about policemen. (story)

f)   I went to two _____ last night. (party)

g)   There are many famous _____ in Europe. (city)

h)   Bob and Jack fight for different _____. (army)

i)   The _____ played together for hours. (boy)

Singular noun ending in 's', 'ss', 'ch' or 'x'

If the noun ends in 's', 'ss', 'ch' or 'x', we generally add 'es' to form the plural, for example fox, foxes, but there are exceptions (for example stomach, stomachs).

9 Write the plural of the word in brackets.

a)   My friend put the _____ on the floor. (box)

b)   There are four _____ in this street. (church)

c)   I bought two new _____ yesterday. (watch)

d)   This shop sells the most beautiful _____ . (dress)

e)   I was so hungry I ate two _____ . (lunch)

14

f) Shannon catches two _____ to work every day. (bus)

g) The _____ of the tree are hitting my window. (branch)

h) The shop assistant put the _____ on the shelf. (peach)

i) Lara dropped the _____ on the floor. (glass)

j) Daniel hid behind the _____ . (bush)

Singular noun ending in 'o'

If the noun ends in 'o':

- which is preceded by a vowel, add 's' to form the plural, for example cuckoo, cuckoos.

- which is preceded by a consonant, we generally add 'es' to form the plural, for example tomato, tomatoes, but there are exceptions (for example piano, pianos).

10 Change the noun in the brackets into a plural noun.

a) Jessie ate three _____ for dinner. (potato)

b) I sold two _____ yesterday. (stereo)

c) My friend is frightened of _____ . (volcano)

d) _____ are native to Australia. (kangaroo)

e) The tourists took lots of _____ . (photo)

f) 'You are all _____ ,' shouted the President. (hero)

g) Todd looked at the _____ in the shop. (radio)

h) I went to the supermarket and looked at the different _____ . (shampoo)

Singular noun ending in 'f' or 'fe'

If the noun ends in 'f' or 'fe', we generally change the 'f' to 'v' and add 'es' to form the plural, for example shelf, shelves, but there are exceptions (for example chief, chiefs, and roof, roofs).

11 Choose the best answer.

a) Helen bought the _____ from the shop.

   i) knifes   ii) knives

b) Kevin swept up all of the tree's _____ .

   i) leafs   ii) leaves

c) People say that cats have nine _____ .

   i) lives   ii) lifes

d) Charlotte baked three _____ for the party.

   i) loaves   ii) loafs

e) Ben folded the _____ .

   i) handkerchiefs   ii) handkerchieves

12 Now complete the sentences by changing the singular verb in brackets into its plural form.

a) 'Two _____ make one whole,' said the teacher. (half)

b) The _____ leapt at the sheep. (wolf)

c) Sandy could hear the horses' _____ on the ground. (hoof)

d) Snow White lived with seven _____ before she married the prince. (dwarf)

e) The rich man ran away from the _____ . (thief)

16

Other plural forms

For some singular nouns there is no set rule to follow when forming the plural, for example tooth, teeth (one tooth, two teeth) and man, men (one man, two men). Sometimes the plural is the same as the singular, for example one sheep, two sheep, or one deer, two deer.

13 Underline the correct plural for each noun.

a) woman

    i) women   ii) womans

b) mouse

    i) mouses   ii) mice

c) goose

    i) gees   ii) geese

d) child

    i) children   ii) childers

e) foot

    i) feet   ii) foots

14 How many nouns can you find? Underline each noun.

Christine and Belinda had been invited to a wedding, so they decided to go shopping. The shop they entered looked very nice. Christine tried on a dress and a hat. Belinda tried on a jacket and a skirt. However, the clothes were too expensive so they did not buy anything. All day they shopped but they had no luck. Finally, they both bought something, and on Saturday they went to the wedding. They entered the church and looked at the guests. Oh no! A girl had the dress Christine was wearing and the bride's mother had a blouse like Belinda's!

When did you last go shopping? Where did you go? Who did you go with? What did you buy? Write a short story and count how many nouns you have used.

Uncount nouns

Uncount nouns are nouns that cannot be counted.
They do not have a plural form, for example **milk**.

We can say 'milk' but we cannot say 'a milk' or 'two milks'.

Some other uncount nouns are

grass water bread luck equipment paper money
ice work rain food protection

Uncount nouns take a singular verb.

- **Water is** good for your health.
- **Music is** popular.

Uncount nouns cannot be used with a/an or a number, but they can be used with the/this/that/my, and so on.

- He gave her **some money**.
- **The ice** is cold.
- **My grass** is green.
- **That bread** is fresh.

15 Complete the sentences using the uncount nouns in the box below.

wood   water   equipment   snow   money
hair   breakfast

a) The _____ is white and cold.

b) I got this _____ from my job.

c) She pulled her _____ away from her face.

d) I drank some _____ .

e) Daniel will use the _____ for the fire.

f) Tim bought some _____ for the office.

g) He was hungry so he ate his _____ .

Pronouns

Pronouns are used to replace nouns in a sentence. By using pronouns, we do not have to repeat the same noun many times. Pronouns make speaking and writing clearer and quicker.

'He' is a pronoun. In this sentence it stands for Jack.

Jack likes money. **He** has $6000.

For example, in the following sentence 'he' and 'her' are both pronouns.

When George held the baby girl and saw **her** smile **he** felt very happy.

If we did not use pronouns we would have to say this:

When George held the baby girl and saw **the baby girl** smile **George** felt very happy.

These words are all pronouns:

Singular	Plural
I	we
you	you
he, she, it	they
me	us
you	you
him, her, it	them
mine	ours
yours	yours
his, hers, its	theirs

1 Underline the pronouns in the following sentences.

a) I weigh 67 kilograms.

b) She has blue sneakers.

c) You have nice hair.

d) They swim every day.

e) He likes to eat chocolate.

f) We wear hats in summer.

g) Have you seen her new haircut?

h) They gave us a lovely Christmas present.

i) She asked me to watch him.

j) Will you put it away?

2 Underline the pronouns in the following story.

Rebecca and Jacob bought some fish and chips for lunch yesterday. We asked them for some, but they told us they didn't have enough for everyone. However, when they had finished there were some chips left over. They gave the chips to Fiona. She felt very happy. Then they all went and watched TV together.

3 Fill in the gaps in the following sentences and underline the noun that is replaced by the pronoun. The first one has been done for you.

a) Daniel is clever. We will ask ___him___ to talk to the class.

b) Duncan and Ben are working hard. I will cook muffins for _____ .

c) Tom has some books. _____ is looking for _____ .

d)   My cat is called Suzy. _____ likes to chase stones.

e)   Have you seen the new movie? I like _____ very much.

f)   Where are my sneakers? Have you seen _____ ?

g)   Our family is going on holiday. _____ are very excited.

h)   My wife and I love gardening. _____ have a very big garden.

i)   When Jim's car was stopped by the police _____ felt nervous.

j)   My daughter is playing the piano. _____ friends are listening.

4 Choose the best answer for each sentence.

a)   The cat licked _____ paws.
   i)   its   ii)   it

b)   Rebecca was lonely so she asked _____ to visit.
   i)   he   ii)   him

c)   I cut my finger when _____ was preparing the vegetables.
   i)   I   ii)   me

d)   The dog was naughty. _____ ran away from _____ .
   i)   it, me   ii)   me, it

e)   The journey was long. _____ took _____ three hours.
   i)   we, it   ii)   it, us

f)   _____ does not enjoy swimming. _____ prefers basketball.
   i)   Lucy. She   ii)   Mary and Lucy, They

g)   _____ do not listen to me. I cannot make _____ do us I say.
   i)   They, them   ii)   He, him

h)   'Oh no! He is talking about _____ holiday again!'
   i)   his   ii)   him

i)   Michael called _____ last night. _____ talked for two hours.

    i)   I, They   ii)   me, We

j)   _____ hurt his knee. The doctor told _____ to rest for six weeks.

    i)   He, him   ii)   His, him

5 Choose the best answer for each sentence.

a)   I decided to ask _____ to the cinema.

    i)   she   ii)   her

b)   _____ told me that the movie was good.

    i)   He   ii)   Him

c)   I looked for _____ number in the phone book.

    i)   her   ii)   he

d)   My grandmother asked _____ to sing.

    i)   I   ii)   me

e)   We talked to a friend of _____ at school yesterday.

    i)   ours   ii)   us

f)   I left _____ jumper at home. May I borrow one of _____ ?

    i)   my, yours   ii)   mine, your

g)   I felt proud of Bill when _____ won the award.

    i)   he   ii)   him

h)   They enjoyed talking to _____ at the wedding.

    i)   she   ii)   her

i)   This shop is too expensive for _____ . Let us go somewhere else.

    i)   we   ii)   us

j)   _____ went shopping with _____ this morning.

    i)   I, him   ii)   Her, me

Adjectives

Adjectives give you more information about a noun or pronoun. They are sometimes called 'describing words'. They answer the question, 'What is (the noun) like?'

> The man was wearing **black** shoes and a **big** hat.

This word tells you about the shoes.

This word tells you about the hat.

An adjective usually comes before a noun but it can also come afterwards.

Ben looked **frightened**.

adjective

He is **fast**.

adjective

More adjectives:

> large   small   tall   huge   thin   blue   yellow   green   dark
> angry   hot   happy   unhappy   pretty   beautiful

1 Add an adjective to describe each of these nouns.

a) _____ sky   b) _____ hair

c) _____ truck   d) _____ pen

e) _____ car   f) _____ shop

g) _____ paper   h) _____ flower

i) _____ woman   j) _____ house

k) _____ tree   l) _____ jacket

m) _____ desk   n) _____ newspaper

2 Draw a (circle) around the adjectives in these sentences.

a) My friend is funny and kind.

b) Today she is wearing a pink dress.

c) She has a green bag.

d) Her hair is long and straight.

e) She has a big dog called Spike.

f) I think she is beautiful.

g) The friendly man asked her to help him carry his heavy bag.

h) She walked up the steep green hill.

i) Her name is Jan and she has white skin, black hair and long legs.

j) She lives in a small house with her mother and father.

This is a friendly lion

3 Draw a (circle) around the adjectives in these sentences.

a) 'This chocolate is yummy,' said the boy.

b) The grey shark swam through the deep water.

c) James walked slowly through the busy airport.

d) My teacher gives us difficult homework sometimes.

e) I bought a delicious chocolate bar yesterday.

f) My mother is reading a good book at the moment.

g) The little boy ate a long worm.

h) The toy is small, white and fluffy.

i) 'This room is dark and messy,' said my angry mother.

j) The strong man lifted the heavy box off the ground.

Read this story.

My house

'This is my house,' said Bill. 'It is made of white bricks. It has four big bedrooms and two bathrooms. One bathroom is quite big and one bathroom is quite small. The kitchen is blue. There is a large bench in it for cooking. Our garden is wonderful. It has lots of green trees for me to play in. My father and I built a small playhouse in one of the trees. There is also a white swing and many beautiful flowers. I think I am a very lucky boy.'

What is your house like? Write about it here:

Comparison of adjectives

There are three different forms of adjectives that we use when we want to make comparisons.

1 The **positive** is the simple form of the adjective, for example:

Charles is **small**.

2 The **comparative** compares two nouns, for example:

Bill is **smaller** than Charles.

3 The **superlative** shows the highest form of the adjective. It compares at least three nouns, for example:

Jane is the **smallest** of all three.

Charles

Bill

Jane

Charles is **small**. (Positive)	Bill is **smaller** than Charles. (Comparative)	Jane is the **smallest** of all three. (Superlative)

To make the comparative adjective we generally add 'er' to the positive adjective, for example:

small ──▶ small**er**

To make the superlative adjective we generally add 'est' to the positive adjective, for example:

small ──▶ small**est**

If the adjective ends in 'y' we need to change it to 'i' before adding 'er' or 'est', for example:

pretty ──▶ prett **i er** ──▶ prett **i est**

Some long adjectives don't use 'er' or 'est'. Instead, we simply add 'more' or 'the most' before the adjective, for example:

beautiful ──▶ **more** beautiful ──▶ **the most** beautiful

For other adjectives, the comparative and superlative are completely different words, for example:

good ──▶ better ──▶ best   bad ──▶ worse ──▶ worst

4 Put the adjectives below in the correct columns.

	Positive	Comparative	Superlative
a)			
b)			
c)			
d)			
e)			
f)			

a) big   bigger   biggest

b) smarter   smart   smartest

c) dirty   dirtier   dirtiest

d) happiest   happier   happy

e) hotter   hottest   hot

f) dark   darkest   darker

5 Complete the table below.

	Positive	Comparative	Superlative
a)	bright		
b)	funny		
c)	interesting		
d)		sweeter	
e)	large		
f)			thinnest
g)		friendlier	
h)	dangerous		
i)	good		

6 Complete these sentences by using the adjective provided. Decide if it should be a positive, comparative or superlative adjective.

The first one has been done for you.

a) Banana cake is **yummy** but chocolate cake is _yummier_ .

b) My classmate is **clever** but my teacher is _____ .

c) Bob is **taller** than Jane, but Kate is the _____ .

d) Of all three, Ming is the _____ . (fast)

e) 'Look at that dog! He is _____ than the baby!' (large)

f) My homework was **good** but Joe's was _____ than mine and Susie's was the _____ of all.

7 Write one sentence comparing the two things in each picture. Draw a line under the adjective. The first one has been done for you.

a) The woman is happier than the man.

b) _____

c) _____

d) _____

8 Write one sentence comparing the pictures below. Use a superlative adjective. Draw a (circle) around the adjective you use. The first one has been done for you.

a)   The boy in the middle is the (youngest).

b) _____

c) _____

d) _____

9 Finish the table below.

	Positive	Comparative	Superlative
a)	long	longer	longest
b)	boring		
c)	tall		
d)	honest		
e)	poor		
f)	calm		
g)	different		
h)	green		
i)	clever		
j)	bad		

Verbs

A **verb** is a word, or a group of words, that tells you what someone or something is being or doing. It is often called a 'doing word'. When we talk about verbs, we are talking about the things we do.

These words are all verbs:

write talk eat sleep sing sit run

A **verb** is the most important word in a sentence. Without a verb, a sentence is not complete, for example:

She her tea.	She the shops.

The two sentences above do not make any sense. They have a subject, which is the person or thing doing the action, but they need a verb.

She **drinks** her tea.	She **visits** the shops.

| The word 'she' is the subject. 'She' is the person who drinks. | The word 'drinks' is the verb. | The word 'she' is the subject. 'She' is the person who visits the shops. | The word 'visits' is the verb. |

The action or verb: 'drinks'.

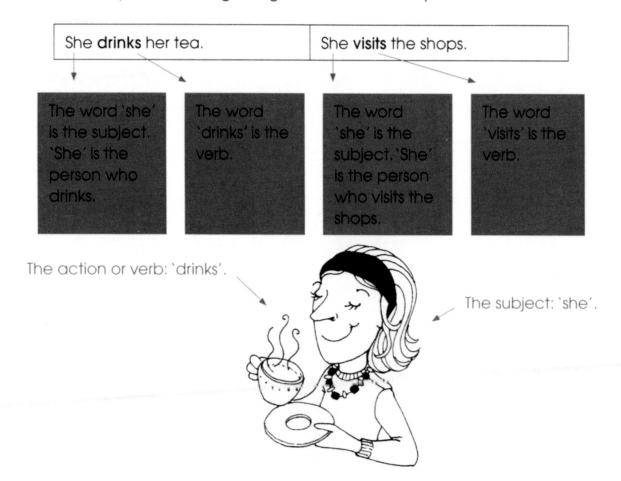

The subject: 'she'.

1 Underline the verb in each sentence.

Breakfast time

a) The alarm rang at six o'clock.

b) Alan got out of bed.

c) The cat bit Rachel's toe.

d) Christine put butter on the bread.

e) Alan read the newspaper.

f) The dog waited at the door.

g) My brother listened to the radio.

h) I brushed my teeth.

i) We all waved goodbye.

j) I walked down the road to school.

> Now you try: write about what happens at breakfast time in your house. Underline the **verbs**.

2 Add a verb to complete each sentence.

a) Lucy _____ a song to her mother.

b) Robert _____ on the television.

c) Mark and Kate _____ to Wellington by bus.

d) The old man _____ down on the chair.

e) They _____ a book together.

f) During the holidays, Rebecca and Joyce _____ (to) many different restaurants.

g) The baby boy _____ his brother.

h) Samantha _____ up the road to join her friends.

i) Bobby _____ out of the window at the rain.

j) The man _____ some food from the shop.

3 Choose the best verb to complete each sentence.

a) She _____ her car to the supermarket.

i) rode   ii) drove

b) The cat _____ the dog.

i) scratched   ii) hit

c) Raewyn _____ flowers for her sick mother.

i) bought   ii) pulled

d) He _____ on the kettle.

i) pushed   ii) turned

e) The teacher _____ the students homework.

i) gave   ii) ate

f)   Sam _____ the walls of the house.

   i)   put   ii)   painted

g)   Greg and Zoe _____ potatoes in their garden.

   i)   planted   ii)   cut

h)   Elizabeth _____ a basketball team.

   i)   won   ii)   joined

i)   He _____ the door and said hello.

   i)   opened   ii)   pushed

j)   She _____ the picture on the wall.

   i)   hung   ii)   thought

Some sentences need only the subject and the verb. For example:

> **Helen smiled.**

In this sentence, 'Helen' is the subject and 'smiled' is the verb.

In other sentences the verb needs to have an object as well. The object tells you what or whom the verb affects. For example:

| John washed the **dishes**. | Natalie liked **Ben**. | Rebecca drank the **orange juice**. |

| Question: John washed what? | Question: Natalie liked whom? | Question: Rebecca drank what? |
| Answer: dishes | Answer: Ben | Answer: orange juice |

The words 'dishes', 'Ben' and 'orange juice' are all objects.

A verb that needs an object is called a **transitive verb**.

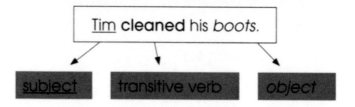

Tim **cleaned** his *boots*.

subject   transitive verb   object

A verb that does not need an object is called an **intransitive verb**.

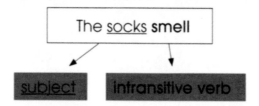

The <u>socks</u> **smell**

subject   intransitive verb

Intransitive verbs can be understood by themselves. They do not need an object.

Some verbs can be both **transitive** and **intransitive**.

Transitive	Intransitive
He smelt the burnt toast.	He smells.
She is playing the piano.	She is playing.

4 Circle the subject in these sentences.

a)   The boss went into the office.

b)   Kay rang the student.

c)   Brian comes from England.

d)   Susan and Lesley studied hard for their exams.

e)   My sister dropped the cup.

5 Underline the object in these sentences.

a)   She wore a bracelet.

b)   Helen ate all the strawberries.

c)   Bob rang the business for information.

d)   The police officer stopped the man.

e)   The roast lamb was burnt by the chef.

6 Add a subject to complete each sentence.

a)   The _____ flew the plane into the sky.

b)   _____ is very interesting.

c)   The _____ was three hours long.

d)   _____ is watching television.

e)   _____ and _____ are from Canada.

7 Add an object to complete each sentence.

a)   The man drove a _____ .

b)   Hannah ran around the _____ .

c)   Hazel baked _____ .

d)   She read _____ .

e)   Karen and Sylvia held onto _____ .

Subject and verb agreement

The subject tells us who or what does the action of the verb.

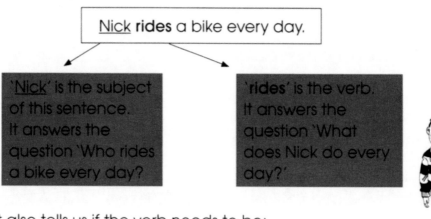

Nick **rides** a bike every day.

'Nick' is the subject of this sentence. It answers the question 'Who rides a bike every day?'

'**rides**' is the verb. It answers the question 'What does Nick do every day?'

one person

The subject also tells us if the verb needs to be:

- singular — about one person, place or thing

or

- plural — about two or more people, places or things.

two or more people

> Note that most nouns form their plurals by adding 's' (see Nouns chapter) but most verbs form their singular by adding 's', for example 'barks' is the singular form ('the dog barks').

The verb must agree with the subject:

If the subject is singular, the verb must also be singular.

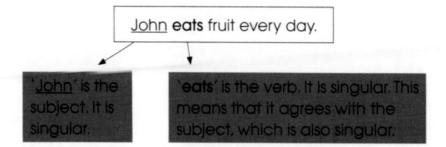

John **eats** fruit every day.

'John' is the subject. It is singular.

'**eats**' is the verb. It is singular. This means that it agrees with the subject, which is also singular.

Answers

Pages 4–5

1 a) an
  b) a
  c) a
  d) an
  e) an

2 a) an
  b) a
  c) The
  d) a, the
  e) an, the
  f) a, The
  g) a
  h) a
  i) a
  j) a, the

Page 5

3 a) some
  b) some
  c) some
  d) some, the
  e) some, The
  f) some
  g) The
  h) The
  i) some, The
  j) The

Page 7

1 a) i
  b) i
  c) ii
  d) iii
  e) ii
  f) i
  g) iii
  h) ii
  i) i
  j) iii

Page 8

  Nouns: cup, finger, flower, grass, sock

1 Nouns: box, table, dog, book, girl

Page 9

2 a) Boris, cat, road
  b) Sue, dress
  c) Tom, dog, cat, rabbit, bird
  d) Mary, car
  e) man, bed, table, chair

Pages 10–11

3 a) wife, beach
  b) umbrella, sand
  c) Craig, Lara, basket
  d) Lara, sunscreen, baby
  e) water
  f) Craig, waves
  g) Tameka, sandcastle
  h) Kevin, boat
  i) sandwiches
  j) rocks, fish

4 a) i
  b) ii
  c) ii
  d) iii
  e) iii

Page 11

5 a) Neil
  b) Sunday
  c) England
  d) Christmas
  e) Paula
  f) Easter
  g) Rome
  h) Spain
  i) Mr Mills
  j) Moscow

Page 12

6 a) Friday
  b) Miss Smith
  c) Egypt
  d) John
  e) Nile
  f) England
  g) London
  h) November
  i) Monday

7 A country — Russia
  A month — December
  A person — Michael Jordan
  A day — Wednesday
  A city — London

Pages 14–15

8 a) flies
  b) cherries
  c) babies
  d) turkeys
  e) stories
  f) parties
  g) cities
  h) armies
  i) boys

9 a) boxes
  b) churches
  c) watches
  d) dresses
  e) lunches
  f) buses
  g) branches
  h) peaches
  i) glasses
  j) bushes

Page 15

10 a) potatoes
   b) stereos
   c) volcanoes
   d) kangaroos
   e) photos
   f) heroes
   g) radios
   h) shampoos

Page 16

11 a) ii
   b) ii
   c) i
   d) i
   e) i or ii

12 a) halves
   b) wolves
   c) hooves or hoofs
   d) dwarves
   e) thieves

Page 17

13 a) i
   b) ii
   c) ii
   d) i
   e) i

14 Christine and Belinda had been invited to a wedding, so they decided to go shopping. The shop they entered looked very nice. Christine tried on a dress and a hat. Belinda tried on a jacket and a skirt. However, the clothes were too expensive so they did not buy anything. All day they shopped but they had no luck. Finally, they both bought something, and on Saturday they went to the wedding. They entered the church and looked at the guests. Oh no! A girl had the dress Christine was wearing and the bride's mother had a blouse like Belinda's!

Page 19

15 a) snow
   b) money
   c) hair
   d) water
   e) wood
   f) equipment
   g) breakfast

Pages 21–22

1 a) i
  b) She
  c) You
  d) They
  e) He
  f) We
  g) you, her
  h) They, us
  i) She, me, him
  j) you, it

2 Rebecca and Jacob bought some fish and chips for lunch yesterday. We asked them for some, but they told us they didn't have enough for everyone. However, when they had finished there were some chips left over. They gave the chips to Fiona. She felt very happy. Then they all went and watched TV together.

3 b) Duncan and Ben, them
  c) Tom, He, books, them
  d) Suzy, She
  e) movie, It
  f) sneakers, them
  g) Our family, We
  h) My wife and I, We
  i) Jim, he
  j) My daughter, Her

Pages 22–23

4 a) i
  b) ii
  c) i
  d) i
  e) ii

f) i
g) i
h) i
i) ii
j) i

5 a) ii
   b) i
   c) i
   d) ii
   e) i
   f) i
   g) i
   h) ii
   i) ii
   j) i

1 Suggested answers:
   a) blue
   b) long
   c) big
   d) black
   e) fast
   f) good
   g) white
   h) lovely
   i) beautiful
   j) small
   k) tall
   l) yellow
   m) large
   n) old

2 a) funny, kind
   b) pink
   c) green
   d) long, straight
   e) big
   f) beautiful
   g) friendly, heavy
   h) steep, green
   i) white, black, long
   j) small

3 a) yummy
   b) grey, deep
   c) busy
   d) difficult
   e) delicious
   f) good
   g) little, long
   h) small, white, fluffy
   i) dark, messy, angry
   j) strong, heavy

4 a) big, bigger, biggest
   b) smart, smarter, smartest
   c) dirty, dirtier, dirtiest
   d) happy, happier, happiest
   e) hot, hotter, hottest
   f) dark, darker, darkest

5 a) bright, brighter, brightest
   b) funny, funnier, funniest
   c) interesting, more interesting, most
      interesting
   d) sweet, sweeter, sweetest
   e) large, larger, largest

f) thin, thinner, thinnest
g) friendly, friendlier, friendliest
h) dangerous, more dangerous, most
   dangerous
i) good, better, best

6 b) cleverer
   c) tallest
   d) fastest
   e) larger
   f) better, best

7 Suggested answers
   b) The dog is bigger than the cat.
   c) The boy is dirtier than the girl.
   d) The man is hotter than the boy.

8 Suggested answers:
   b) Arnold is the <u>strongest</u>.
   c) Lily's slice is the <u>largest</u>.
   d) Sarah is the <u>naughtiest</u> student in the
      class.

9 b) boring, more boring, most boring
   c) tall, taller, tallest
   d) honest, more honest, most honest
   e) poor, poorer, poorest
   f) calm, calmer, calmest
   g) different, more different, most
      different
   h) green, greener, greenest
   i) clever, cleverer, cleverest
   j) bad, worse, worst

1 a) rang
   b) got
   c) bit
   d) put
   e) read
   f) waited
   g) listened
   h) brushed
   i) waved
   j) walked

2 Suggested answers:
   a) sang
   b) turned
   c) travelled
   d) sat
   e) read
   f) went
   g) loved
   h) ran
   i) looked
   j) bought

3 a) ii
   b) i
   c) i
   d) ii
   e) i
   f) ii
   g) i
   h) ii
   i) i
   j) i

4 a) boss
   b) Kay
   c) Brian
   d) Susan and Lesley
   e) sister

5 a) bracelet
   b) strawberries
   c) business
   d) man
   e) roast lamb

6 Suggested answers:
   a) pilot
   b) The museum
   c) movie
   d) She
   e) Jack, Jill

7 Suggested answers:
   a) car
   b) park
   c) muffins
   d) a book
   e) the boat

8 a) ii
   b) i
   c) i
   d) ii
   e) i
   f) i
   g) ii
   h) ii
   i) i
   j) ii

9 a) i
   b) ii
   c) i
   d) ii
   e) i
   f) i
   g) ii
   h) ii
   i) i
   j) ii

10 a) hit
   b) made
   c) rang
   d) is talking
   e) bought
   f) ran
   g) has
   h) is
   i) pushed
   j) is running

11 Suggested answers:
   a) ate
   b) saw
   c) wore
   d) caught
   e) went
   f) finish
   g) water
   h) knocked

i) lives
j) went

Page 42

12 b) Subject: Mark. Verb: smiled. Object: wife.
  c) Subject: teacher. Verb: talked. Object: student.
  d) Subject: girl. Verb: watched. Object: TV.
  e) Subject: baby. Verb: played. Object: box.
  f) Subject: dog. Verb: ate. Object: bone.

13 Suggested answers:
  a) a story
  b) the baby
  c) an apple
  d) the man
  e) the patient
  f) The ball

Page 44

14 b) She talked to him yesterday.
  c) She bought a new computer.
  d) Billy put the newspaper on the floor.
  e) Ben put the beans in the pot.
  f) He washed the dog yesterday. Yesterday he washed the dog.
  g) He passed the ball to her.
  h) Megan laughed at the funny joke.
  i) The boat spilled oil into the water.
  j) The policeman studied the tyre marks.

Page 45

15 a) She walked up the road to the park.
  b) The cat waited by the fridge.
  c) The girl carried the baby.
  d) Deborah ate too much cake.
  e) The bird sat in a tree.

16 a) ii
  b) ii
  c) i
  d) i
  e) ii

Pages 46–47

17 b) The girl read the book.
  c) The dog slept on the floor.
  d) Elaine pulled up the rope.
  e) Bill washed the dog.
  f) Lily said she would marry Trevor.
  g) Jeremy cut a slice of cake.
  h) The little mouse hid from the cat.
  i) Gary wanted to be a policeman.
  j) Rebecca shouted at the black cat.
  k) The car went around the corner.
  l) The student passed all of his exams.
  m) Joseph had a party.
  n) Charlie went to school for five years.

Page 47

18 Suggested answers:
  a) She read her email.
  b) Christine cleaned the oven.
  c) Alan drove the van into the garage.
  d) Rachel and Ben won the tennis game last month.
  e) I always go to the library on Saturdays.

f) They will go to Japan for a holiday next month.
g) Tracey put the flowers on the table.
h) We go to the swimming pool every afternoon.
i) Tabitha read a book called *Grammar Games*.

Page 49

1 b) talks, present simple
  c) will go, future
  d) went, past simple
  e) watches, present simple
  f) left, past simple
  g) will go, future
  h) liked, past simple
  i) shouted, past simple
  j) picked, past simple

Page 50

2 Present simple tense verbs:
    comes
    see
    walk
    see
    stay
  Past simple tense verbs:
    took
    stood
    watched
    enjoyed
    told
    were
  Future tense verbs:
    will visit
    will take

Page 51

3 a) knocked
  b) called
  c) shouted
  d) hurried
  e) studied
  f) copied
  g) smiled
  h) left

4 called, shouted, left, hurried, knocked, smiled, studied, copied

Page 53

5

go	went	gone
become	became	become
fight	fought	fought
choose	chose	chosen
blow	blew	blown
make	made	made
light	lit	lit
be	was/were	been
drink	drank	drunk
drive	drove	driven
cost	cost	cost
run	ran	run
sink	sank	sunk
sing	sang	sung
sell	sold	sold
write	wrote	written
lie	lay	lain
wear	wore	worn
take	took	taken
has	had	had
freeze	froze	frozen
fly	flew	flown

Pages 55–56

1 a) happily
  b) loudly
  c) very slowly
  d) Hurriedly
  e) rather quickly
  f) Yesterday
  g) suddenly
  h) sweetly, yesterday

2 a) ii
  b) iii
  c) i
  d) iii
  e) i
  f) ii
  g) iii
  h) iii
  i) ii
  j) iii

Page 56

3 b) Verb: spoke
    Adverb/adverbial phrase: loudly
  c) Verb: raining
    Adverb/adverbial phrase: rather heavily
  d) Verb: jumped
    Adverb/adverbial phrase: Smoothly
  e) Verb: played
    Adverb/adverbial phrase: happily
  f) Verb: built
    Adverb/adverbial phrase: very slowly

Pages 57–58

4 Suggested answers:
  a) The women relaxed quietly.
    Verb: relaxed
    Adverb/adverbial phrase: quietly
  b) Peacefully, the man watched the sun.
    Verb: watched
    Adverb/adverbial phrase: peacefully
  c) Mother served the dinner slowly.
    Verb: served
    Adverb/adverbial phrase: slowly
  d) Bill and Lillian smiled very happily at each other.
    Verb: smiled
    Adverb/adverbial phrase: very happily
  e) Yesterday, Bill and Lillian celebrated their anniversary.
    Verb: celebrated
    Adverb/adverbial phrase: Yesterday
  f) Julia quietly read the book.
    Verb: read
    Adverb/adverbial phrase: quietly

Page 60

5 sadly
  quickly
  angrily
  sleepily

6 a) dangerously
  b) sweetly
  c) Luckily
  d) thankfully
  e) noisily
  f) normally

g) feebly
h) angrily
i) easily
j) poorly

Pages 61-62

1. a) through
   b) into
   c) between
   d) inside
   e) at
   f) to, in
   g) with, on
   h) to, in
   i) to, in
   j) on

Pages 62-63

2. on, under, in, inside, beside, to, for

3. a) i
   b) i
   c) ii
   d) i
   e) i
   f) i
   g) i
   h) i
   i) ii
   j) i

Pages 63-64

4. a) i
   b) i
   c) iii
   d) ii
   e) i
   f) iii
   g) iii
   h) i
   i) ii
   j) ii

Page 64

5. a) ii
   b) i
   c) i
   d) i
   e) i
   f) ii
   g) i
   h) i
   i) i
   j) i

Page 66

1. b) but she has never been to Spain.
   c) but I have not tried kimchi.
   d) and she went to bed.
   e) but I cannot speak French.
   f) and he saw many animals.
   g) but she likes boats.
   h) but I did not understand.
   i) and he goes to the cinema every Saturday.
   j) but she did not pass.

Pages 67-68

2. b) but
   c) and
   d) but
   e) but
   f) but
   g) but
   h) and
   i) and
   j) but

3. Suggested answers:
   a) I did not pass the test.
   b) enjoyed it very much.
   c) he did not pass the test.
   d) she did not finish her degree.
   e) made many friends.
   f) she fell asleep.
   g) it broke.
   h) brushed her teeth.
   i) put it outside.
   j) he did not watch it.

Page 68

4. b) but he is not rich.
   c) but he did not feel cold.
   d) and he ate his breakfast.
   e) and she hurt her knee.
   f) and she felt full.

Pages 70-71

1. a) viii
   b) ix
   c) iv
   d) vi
   e) ii
   f) i
   g) vii
   h) x
   i) iii
   j) v

2. a) I've lost my wallet.
   b) She doesn't want to go.
   c) It wasn't my birthday yesterday.
   d) I think he's found your wallet.
   e) Please hurry or we'll be late.
   f) He isn't very friendly.
   g) They're working in the garden.
   h) I'd better go now.
   i) I won't be late.
   j) I haven't finished my homework.

Page 71

3. is not, isn't
   he will, he'll
   are not, aren't
   does not, doesn't
   we had, we'd
   they would, they'd
   could not, couldn't
   have not, haven't
   I am, I'm
   he is, he's
   you will, you'll
   do not, don't
   cannot, can't
   she is, she's
   you will, you'll
   they have, they've
   they will, they'll
   they had, they'd
   has not, hasn't
   will not, won't

Page 72

4. a) can't
   b) she'd
   c) doesn't
   d) Don't, It's
   e) I'll, he's
   f) hasn't, She'll
   g) He's, He'll
   h) You're
   i) won't, I'm
   j) doesn't

Pages 73-74

5. b) restaurant, Caroline
   c) cake, Lucy
   d) cat, Rachel
   e) car, Jack

Pages 74-75

6. b) Robert's house
   c) Susie's car
   d) Tania's money
   e) Jack's piano

7. a) The dog's water is cold.
   b) Chris's car was slow.
   c) We visited Paris's tower.
   d) Caroline's coat is black.
   e) James's knee is hurt.
   f) David's son is young.
   g) The boss's wife is friendly.
   h) I lost the teacher's book.
   i) She drove to Tim's house.
   j) Ross's farm is large.

Page 75

8. a) The children's teacher is young.
   b) These are the boys' desks.
   c) The women's handbags are lost.
   d) The men's cars are expensive.
   e) These are the horses' combs.
   f) The students' computers are new.
   g) Those are the teachers' offices.
   h) His parents' house is large.
   i) The babies' toys are on the floor.
   j) The girls' dresses are dirty.

Page 76

9. a) The cat's name is Tiger.
   b) Have you met Emma's brothers?
   c) This is Ross's bag.
   d) Thomas's painting is in the art museum.
   e) The man's job is difficult.
   f) My books are in my friend's bag.
   g) The ladies' clothes are beautiful.
   h) The Whites' house is only three years old.
   i) I have three dogs. The dogs' meat is in the freezer.
   j) Charles's homework is very good.

10. a) Those are the teachers' cars.
    b) Bob's shirt is green.
    c) The woman's baby is cute.
    d) Jim's swimming pool is deep.
    e) These are the girls' fathers.
    f) Steven's cushions are ripped.
    g) This is my grandfather's wallet.
    h) The boy's name is Wayne.
    i) Sam is Curtis's friend.

If the subject is plural, the verb must also be plural.

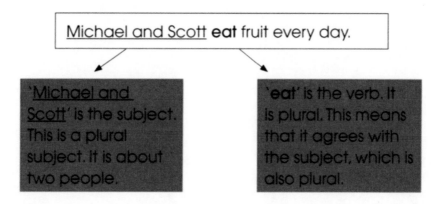

Michael and Scott **eat** fruit every day.

'Michael and Scott' is the subject. This is a plural subject. It is about two people.

'eat' is the verb. It is plural. This means that it agrees with the subject, which is also plural.

The two exceptions are 'I' and 'you' (singular), which are singular subjects that take the same form as a plural verb, for example 'I like', 'you like'.

8 Choose the correct verb to complete each sentence.

a) Rebecca _____ the piano.

i) play   ii) plays

b) My husband _____ his book every night.

i) reads   ii) read

c) He _____ to a restaurant every Saturday.

i) goes   ii) go

d) My neighbour _____ very loudly.

i) sing   ii) sings

e) The office _____ large.

i) is   ii) are

f) She _____ faster than Teresa.

i) runs   ii) run

g) Cats can _____ faster than mice.

    i) runs   ii) run

h) Alan _____ very hard.

    i) work   ii) works

i) I think they _____ coming!

    i) are   ii) is

j) Her grandmother _____ every week.

    i) visit   ii) visits

9 Choose the correct verb to complete each sentence.

a) They _____ here every week to watch a movie.

    i) come   ii) comes

b) He _____ home after ten o'clock.

    i) go   ii) goes

c) The students _____ playing sport.

    i) enjoy   ii) enjoys

d) Amy and Stuart _____ neighbours.

    i) is   ii) are

e) The children _____ listening to music.

    i) like   ii) likes

f) Sarah _____ bananas and tomatoes.

    i) hates   ii) hate

g) They _____ going shopping tomorrow.

    i) is   ii) are

h) The man _____ people how to drive.

    i) teach   ii) teaches

i) That restaurant _____ delicious food.

     i) has   ii) have

j) They _____ married at three o'clock.

     i) was   ii) were

10 Circle the verb in each of these sentences.

a) Sophie hit her brother on the hand.

b) Lara made a cake for her daughter.

c) Beverley rang Brenda last night.

d) The doctor is talking to the patient.

e) He bought a new computer for his business.

f) Duncan and Ben ran into the driveway.

g) Michael has ten toy trucks in his cupboard.

h) She is a very good friend of mine.

i) David pushed the box down the stairs.

j) Ben is running in the race.

11 Complete each sentence by adding a suitable verb.

a) The cat _____ the food.

b) Penny _____ her house.

c) Graham and Michael _____ their new jackets to the sports game.

d) The fisherman _____ a huge fish.

e) My friend _____ to China.

f) Did you _____ your homework?

g) You need to _____ the plants.

h) Gary _____ on the door.

i) She _____ on Checko Street.

j) We _____ to see a movie last night.

12 Find the subject (s), verb (v) and object (o) in these sentences. The first one has been done for you.

         (s) (v)   (o)

a) The girl ate an apple.

b) Mark smiled at his wife.

c) The teacher talked to the student.

d) The girl watched the TV.

e) The baby played with the box.

f) The dog ate the bone.

13 Now you finish these sentences by adding an object.

a) Mandy wrote _____ .

b) Susan's mother watched _____ .

c) Shannon was eating _____ .

d) The friends waved to _____ .

e) The doctor talked to _____ .

f) _____ was kicked by the football player.

Sentence order

Use these words to make new sentences. You will need to add extra words so the sentences make sense. For example:

The **dog sat** on the **floor**.

Subjects	Verbs	Objects
bird	eat	cat
friend	talked	friend
mother	sat	chair
I	phoned	father
students	smile	floor
dog	drove	tree
boy	sang	bed
Jane	slept	movie
teacher	watches	car
woman	climbs	John
he	washed	song
she	cleans	hamburger

a)   the bone the dog ate.

The dog ate the bone.

b)   talked she him to yesterday.

c)   bought a she computer new.

d)   newspaper the on Billy put the floor.

e)   Ben in the pot the put beans.

f)   yesterday he dog the washed.

g)   ball to passed he the her.

h)   funny joke Megan laughed at the.

i)   boat spilled the water into the oil.

j)   tyre marks policeman studied the the.

a) walked up road the to the park she

_____

b) the fridge the cat waited by

_____

c) carried the girl the baby

_____

d) Deborah too cake ate much

_____

e) The bird a tree sat in

_____

a) i) Kevin has caught. ☐

 ii) Kevin has caught a fish. ☐

b) i) Mum a present under the Christmas tree. ☐

 ii) Mum put a present under the Christmas tree. ☐

c) i) Patricia read a story in the newspaper. ☐

 ii) Patricia a story. ☐

d) i) Susan lit the candle on the cake. ☐

 ii) Susan the candle on the cake. ☐

e) i) She to the shop. ☐

 ii) She went to the shop. ☐

17 Change the word order in these sentences so they are correct. Remember to use a capital letter at the beginning of each sentence and a full stop at the end. The first one has been done for you.

a)   a of piece Ben ate chocolate

Ben ate a piece of chocolate.

b)   girl the the book read

c)   dog slept on the the floor

d)   the Elaine rope up pulled

e)   the dog Bill washed

f)   said she marry Lily Trevor would

g)   Jeremy cut slice cake of a

h)   little the hid cat from mouse the

i)   wanted to Gary a be policeman

j)   shouted Rebecca at cat the black

k)   car went cornor around the the

l)   student exams all passed of his the

_____

m)   Joseph party had a

_____

n)   school went to Charlie years five for

_____

18 Add one or two words to complete each sentence.

a)   She her email.

_____

b)   Christine the oven.

_____

c)   Alan the van into the garage.

_____

d)   Rachel and Ben the tennis game last month.

_____

e)   I always the library on Saturdays.

_____

f)   They to Japan for a holiday next month.

_____

g)   Tracey the flowers on the table.

_____

h)   We the swimming pool every afternoon.

_____

i)   Tabitha a book called *Grammar Games*.

_____

Tenses: when things happen

Remember that a verb tells us what a person or thing is doing. Every verb needs to have a **tense** because this shows when the verb (or action) happens.

Present simple tense: now

The **present simple tense** is used to talk about things that happen in general, often, repeatedly.

Daniel and Jacob **walk** to school.

This means that Daniel and Jacob walk to school together often.

We must say: I, we, you, they   walk, drive, talk

he, she, it   walks, drives, talks

They walk to school. He drives his car.

Past simple tense: before

The **past tense** is used to talk about things that happened at a time that is finished, past, some time ago.

Daniel and Jacob **walked** to school.

This means that Daniel and Jacob walked to school earlier today, yesterday, last month or last year … sometime in the past.

When using the past tense, 'ed' is usually added to the verb to show the different time used. For example: walk ⟶ walked

If the verb ends in 'y', change the 'y' to 'i' and add 'ed' to form the past tense. For example: cry ⟶ cried

48

However, there are some verbs where the past tense is created by changing the word. For example:

begin ⟶ began

write ⟶ wrote

speak ⟶ spoke

These verbs are called irregular verbs.

Future tense: next

The **future tense** is used to talk about things that will happen some time in the future, for example tomorrow, next year or later in the day.

Daniel and Jacob **will walk** to school this morning.

1 Now you try: underline the verbs in each sentence, and write whether it is in the present simple, past simple or future tense. The first one has been done for you.

a)	She <u>started</u> the company five years ago.	past simple
b)	Mum talks to her best friend every day.	
c)	I will go to Hong Kong for my holiday this year.	
d)	Last year I went to England for Christmas.	
e)	My sister watches TV after school.	
f)	Lesley left school early that day.	
g)	He will go to the library on Tuesday.	
h)	Alan liked the movie.	
i)	She shouted at her boyfriend.	
j)	They picked some flowers.	

2 Find all the verbs in the story and list them in the correct column below. (Note that the plural of 'kiwi' is 'kiwi'.)

The kiwi

The kiwi bird comes from New Zealand. One day our teacher took us to the zoo to see some kiwi. We stood quietly in the dark room and watched them walk around. We enjoyed it very much. I told my family about it. They were very interested. We will visit the zoo again on Saturday so my family can see the kiwi too. We will take our lunch so we can stay all day.

Present simple tense verbs	Past simple tense verbs	Future tense verbs

Present tense of 'to be'		Past tense of 'to be'	
Singular	**Plural**	**Singular**	**Plural**
I am (I'm)	we are (we're)	I was	we were
you are (you're)	you are (you're)	you were	you were
he is (he's) she is (she's) it is (it's)	they are (they're)	he was she was it was	they were
I am hungry. My father is very clever. He is a teacher. We worked very hard. We are tired now.		I was late to school yesterday. It was a funny movie. You were angry this morning.	

Present tense of 'to have'		Past tense of 'to have'	
Singular	**Plural**	**Singular**	**Plural**
I have (I've)	we have (we've)	I had (I'd)	we had (we'd)
you have (you've)	you have (you've)	you had (you'd)	you had (you'd)
he has (he's) she has (she's) it has (it's)	they have (they've)	he had (he'd) she had (she'd) it had (it'd)	they had (they'd)
I have finished my homework. They have fallen asleep. I think my watch is broken. It has stopped.		I had a banana for lunch. We had a holiday last year. She had a good job.	

3 Write the past simple tense verbs on the lines.

a) knock _____   b) call _____

c) shout _____   d) hurry _____

e) study _____   f) copy _____

g) smile _____   h) leave _____

4 Now use the past simple tense verbs from question 3 to complete this story.

One day I was at home eating dinner when Joseph _____

me on the telephone. He _____ at me very loudly, and asked

me to hurry to his house. I _____ my dinner on the table and

_____ to his house. I _____ on the door. Joseph

opened it and _____, then took me into his lounge and told

me what his problem was. I couldn't believe it! He had _____

so hard for his English test that his teacher had come to visit, believing

that he had _____ my work!

What did you do yesterday? Write three sentences using the past simple tense. Underline the verbs. For example:

I ate a big dinner.

1) _____

   _____

2) _____

   _____

3) _____

   _____

What do you do often? Write two sentences using the present simple tense. Underline the verbs. For example:

I talk to my classmate.

1) _____

   _____

2) _____

   _____

What will you do tomorrow? Write three sentences using the future tense. Underline the verbs. For example:

I will go to the cinema.

1) _____

   _____

2) _____

   _____

3) _____

   _____

5 Complete the table of irregular verbs.

Present (infinitive)	Past simple	Past participle
go	went	gone
become		
fight		
	chose	
		blown
	made	
light		
be		
		drunk
	drove	
		cost
	ran	
		sunk
sing		
		sold
write		
lie		
	wore	
		taken
	had	
freeze		
	flew	

Adverbs

An **adverb** qualifies (affects) a verb, an adjective or another adverb. Its job is to give you more information.

Some adverbs describe manner. They tell you how something happened.

> He ran **quickly**.

Some adverbs describe place. They tell you where something happened.

> He ran **around**.

Some adverbs describe time. They tell you when something happened.

> **Afterwards**, he ran.

Adverbs can be one word or a group of words. When there is a group of words we call it an **adverbial group**.

> I am eating **very slowly**.

'very slowly' is the adverbial group.

> The dog is barking **too loudly**.

'too loudly' is the adverbial group.

The words 'very' and 'too' are sometimes called **modifiers** because they modify the second adverb.

a) She ran happily into her parents' room.

b) The boy clapped his hands loudly.

c) He wrote it down very slowly.

d) Hurriedly, they picked up their books.

e) The basketball player passed the ball rather quickly.

f) Yesterday, they went swimming in the sea.

g) Susie suddenly fell on the floor.

h) Mark smiled sweetly at the baby yesterday.

2 Choose the best adverb to complete each sentence.

a) We must leave _____ or we will be late for the movie.

   i) always   ii) soon   iii) slowly

b) The robber crept _____ through the window.

   i) loudly   ii) sadly   iii) quietly

c) The dog ate the food _____.

   i) hungrily   ii) softly   iii) tomorrow

d) The boy ran _____ in a circle.

   i) down   ii) up   iii) around

e) He read the story _____.

   i) quickly   ii) soon   iii) busily

f) The runner sprinted _____ down the track.

   i) quietly   ii) rapidly   iii) slowly

g) The baby cried _____.

   i) silently   ii) happily   iii) loudly

h) Jean shouted _____ at her husband.

    i) happily   ii) softly   iii) angrily

i) Gail closed her eyes _____ .

    i) coolly   ii) tightly   iii) loudly

j) David studied _____ .

    i) neatly   ii) loudly   iii) silently

3 Find the verbs and adverbs in these sentences. The first one has been done for you.

a) The man drove the car quickly.

Verb   drove

Adverb/adverbial phrase   quickly

b) The teacher spoke loudly to the class.

Verb _____

Adverb/adverbial phrase _____

c) It was raining rather heavily last night.

Verb _____

Adverb/adverbial phrase _____

d) Smoothly, the horse jumped over the fence.

Verb _____

Adverb/adverbial phrase _____

e) The girl played happily under the tree.

Verb _____

Adverb/adverbial phrase _____

f) The baby built the sandcastle very slowly.

Verb _____

Adverb/adverbial phrase _____

4 Now write your own sentences. Write your verb and adverb/adverbial phrase in the box beside each picture.

Verb
_____

Adverb/adverbial phrase
_____
_____
_____

a) _____
_____

Verb
_____

Adverb/adverbial phrase
_____
_____
_____

b) _____
_____

Verb
_____

Adverb/adverbial phrase
_____
_____
_____

c) _____
_____

Verb
_____

Adverb/adverbial phrase
_____

_____

d) _____

_____

Verb
_____

Adverb/adverbial phrase
_____

_____

e) _____

_____

Verb
_____

Adverb/adverbial phrase
_____

_____

f) _____

_____

Adverbs are usually made by adding the letters 'ly' to an adjective.

- If the adjective ends in 'y', we generally change it to 'i' and add 'ly', for example noisy, noisily, but there are exceptions (for example coy, coyly).

- If the adjective ends in 'e', we generally add 'ly', for example sure, surely, but there are exceptions (for example gentle, gently).

- If the adjective already ends in 'l' we generally add 'ly', for example hopeful, hopefully, but there are exceptions (for example full, fully).

It is **slow**.

The word 'slow' is an adjective.

It is moving **slowly**.

The word 'slowly' is an adverb. It describes the verb 'moving'.

She is **happy**.

The word 'happy' is an adjective.

She is smiling **happily**.

The word 'happily' is an adverb. It describes the verb 'smiling'.

However, some words do not follow these rules. As you can see in the examples below, the adverb can be the same word as the adjective, or it can be a different word.

Adjective	Adverb
good	well
late	late
early	early
fast	fast
hard	hard

Adjective	Adverb
sad	
quick	
angry	
sleep	

6 Create adverbs to complete the sentences below using the adjectives in brackets.

a)   She likes to drive _____ . (dangerous)

b)   The baby smiled _____ at the nurse. (sweet)

c)   _____ , she found her bag near the door. (lucky)

d)   She picked up the bag _____ . (thankful)

e)   The cars raced _____ around the track. (noisy)

f)   The crazy boy never acts _____ . (normal)

g)   Catherine fell down _____ . (feeble)

h)   Mrs Brown shouted _____ at the students. (angry)

i)   Ben completed the test _____ . (easy)

j)   'You write very _____ ,' said the employer. (poor)

Prepositions

Prepositions are words that show the relationship between words in a sentence. They can indicate place (where), time (when) or manner (how).

A preposition is generally followed by a noun or pronoun.

Where are the ants?

> The ants are **on** the chair.

'On' is a preposition. It shows the relationship between the ants and the chair.

These words are also prepositions:

down through to across into under over inside for since in between on up before at from for about towards with beside

For example:

The woman swam **towards** the drowning man.

He hit the ball **over** the volleyball net.

The criminal was put **in** jail.

He put the food **on** the plate.

1 Underline the prepositions in the following sentences.

a) The cat ran through the door.

b) The young boy jumped into the swimming pool.

c) He parked his car between the trees.

d) Inside that room there is a beautiful painting.

e) My husband visited me at lunchtime.

f) We drove to the beach in my friend's car.

g) I sat with my wife on the aeroplane.

h) We took our books to the library in the city.

i) Before I came to New Zealand I lived in Korea.

j) After the game the basketball player lay down on her bed.

2 <u>Underline</u> the prepositions in the story below.

A lost book!

'I cannot find my book,' said Shannon.

'Have you looked on the table?' Alan asked.

'Yes, and I looked under the table too. I also looked in my bedroom and inside the drawer.'

'Did you look beside the TV?'

'Yes. I hope I find it soon. A friend gave it to me for my birthday last year.'

Alan smiled. 'Well, keep looking!'

3 Choose the best answer for each sentence.

a) Christine is an old friend _____ school.

   i) from   ii) of

b) Switzerland is famous _____ its chocolate.

   i) for   ii) about

c) I am looking for the best car _____ the market.

   i) in   ii) on

d) This book is similar _____ the other one.

   i) to   ii) with

e) I put the flowers _____ the vase.

   i) in   ii) on

f)   Alan let the cat _____ the house.

    i)   in   ii)   out

g)   The cat ran _____ its dinner bowl.

    i)   to   ii)   on   iii)   about

h)   He died _____ old age.

    i)   of   ii)   about   iii)   for

i)   They arrived home _____ 21 January.

    i)   in   ii)   on   iii)   at

j)   'Congratulations _____ your engagement!'

    i)   on   ii)   for   iii)   in

4 Choose the best answer for each of these sentences.

a)   She sat down _____ the chair.

    i)   on   ii)   at   iii)   to

b)   I put the car keys _____ the table.

    i)   on   ii)   in   iii)   to

c)   Tim went _____ the cinema _____ his friend.

    i)   in, to   ii)   to, at   iii)   to, with

d)   He bought flowers _____ her.

    i)   at   ii)   for   iii)   until

e)   Cathy put the book _____ the ground.

    i)   on   ii)   to   iii)   for

f)   Brenda smiled happily _____ her husband.

    i)   in   ii)   from   iii)   at

g)   Maria travelled _____ Los Angeles _____ New York.

    i)   in, at   ii)   to, on   iii)   from, to

h)   Ben waited _____ home for her _____ arrive.

    i)   at, to   ii)   in, to   iii)   for, on

i) She put the cat _____ the ground.

    i)   at   ii)   on   iii)   of

j) We are leaving _____ Tokyo next week.

    i)   to   ii)   for   iii)   about

5   Choose the best answer for each sentence.

a) He smiled _____ me.

    i)   to   ii)   at   iii)   for

b) This necklace is made _____ gold.

    i)   of   ii)   with   iii)   by

c) My parents live _____ a farm.

    i)   on   ii)   in   iii)   within

d) Your teacher will be back _____ an hour.

    i)   within   ii)   about   iii)   on

e) My wife fell _____ a ladder.

    i)   off   ii)   inside   iii)   in

f) My son laughed _____ me.

    i)   of   ii)   at   iii)   from

g) John went _____ Zambia alone.

    i)   to   ii)   at   iii)   in

h) _____ his way to Ireland he stopped over in Singapore.

    i)   On   ii)   In   iii)   at

i) Have you bought a birthday present _____ her?

    i)   for   ii)   to   iii)   with

j) _____ rainy days I usually stay at home.

    i)   On   ii)   In   iii)   At

Conjunctions

The words 'and' and 'but' are called conjunctions.

and

We use 'and' to join two events.

He opened the door. He walked inside.

> He opened the door **and** walked inside.

Sarah woke up. Sarah got out of bed.

> Sarah woke up **and** got out of bed.

The man smiled. The man waved his hand.

> The man smiled **and** waved his hand.

but

We use 'but' to join events when we do not expect the second event.

John was clever. John failed the test.

> John was clever **but** he failed the test.

She was happy. She did not smile.

> She was happy **but** she did not smile.

Frank was rich. Frank was not happy.

> Frank was rich **but** he was not happy.

a) It is winter <u>and it is very cold.</u>

b) She speaks Spanish _____

c) I like Korean food _____

d) She was tired _____

e) I live in Paris _____

f) Jack went to the zoo _____

g) Mary cannot swim _____

h) I listened carefully _____

i) Tim loves watching movies _____

j) Cindy cheated in the test _____

but she did not pass.

but I have not tried kimchi.

and she went to bed.

but I did not understand.

and he saw many animals.

and it is very cold.

but she likes boats.

but she has never been to Spain.

and he goes to the cinema every Saturday.

but I cannot speak French.

a) I went to the shop ___but___ I did not buy anything.

b) Bob was tired _____ he went to work.

c) She shut the door _____ she locked it.

d) Sue was tired _____ she did not sleep.

e) The man was rich _____ he lived in a small house.

f) I bought a book _____ I did not read it.

g) James ate the food _____ he did not like it.

h) Jason went on holiday _____ he had a great time.

i) She worked hard _____ she passed the test.

j) The team was good _____ they lost the game.

3 Complete the sentences.

a) I studied hard but _____

b) Tracey watched the movie and _____

c) David learned how to drive but _____

d) Kim went to university but _____

e) She loved school and _____

f) Lyn went to the party but _____

g) She dropped the glass and _____

h) Christine washed her face and _____

i)   She picked up the rubbish and _____

j)   Ben turned on the television but _____

a)   He loves her but he will not marry her. _____

b)   Alfred is clever _____

c)   Stephen walked in the rain _____

d)   He got out of bed _____

e)   Christine fell over _____

f)   Joanne ate the food _____

he is not rich.

she felt full.

he will not marry her.

he ate his breakfast.

he did not feel cold.

she hurt her knee.

a)   _____

b)   _____

c)   _____

d)   _____

e)   _____

The apostrophe

The apostrophe (') is used when we want to contract (join) two words together.

We use the apostrophe (') to replace the missing letter(s).

I am	→	I'm
you are	→	you're
did not	→	didn't
is not	→	isn't
are not	→	aren't

Positive contractions

	'm (am)	's (is or has)	're (are)	've (have)	'll (will)	'd (would or had)
I	I'm			I've	I'll	I'd
he		he's			he'll	he'd
she		she's			she'll	she'd
it		it's			it'll	it'd
you			you're	you've	you'll	you'd
we			we're	we've	we'll	we'd
they			they're	they've	they'll	they'd

Negative contractions

isn't = is not	aren't = are not	wasn't = was not
weren't = were not	don't = do not	doesn't = does not
didn't = did not	haven't = have not	hasn't = has not
hadn't = had not	can't = cannot	couldn't = could not
won't = will not	wouldn't = would not	shan't = shall not

1 Match the long form with its contraction.

a) we will _____   i) we've

b) does not _____   ii) you'll

c) it is _____   iii) she'll

d) would not _____   iv) it's

e) you will _____   v) aren't

f) we have _____   vi) wouldn't

g) is not _____   vii) isn't

h) you are _____   viii) we'll

i) she will _____   ix) doesn't

j) are not _____   x) you're

2 Put the missing apostrophe in the correct place.

a) Ive lost my wallet.

b) She doesnt want to go.

c)   It wasnt my birthday yesterday.

d)   I think hes found your wallet.

e)   Please hurry or well be late.

f)   He isnt very friendly.

g)   Theyre working in the garden.

h)   Id better go now.

i)   I wont be late.

j)   I havent finished my homework.

3 Complete the table of contractions.

is not _____	he will _____
are not _____	does not _____
we had _____	they would _____
could not _____	have not _____
I am _____	he is _____
you will _____	do not _____
cannot _____	she is _____
you will _____	they have _____
they will _____	they had _____
has not _____	will not _____

a) I <u>cannot</u> remember the answer. _____

b) My sister said <u>she would</u> meet me after school. _____

c) The clock <u>does not</u> work. _____

d) <u>Do not</u> open the window. <u>It is</u> cold. _____ _____

e) <u>I will</u> check if <u>he has</u> closed the door. _____

f) Jackie <u>has not</u> finished her lunch. <u>She will</u> be in trouble.

_____

g) <u>He is</u> my friend. <u>He will</u> phone me tonight. _____

h) <u>You are</u> invited to my party. _____

i) I <u>will not</u> come. <u>I am</u> busy. _____

j) Daniel <u>does not</u> like tomatoes. _____

Possession

We often add the possessive ('s) to talk about things that belong to people or animals.

Whose book is it?

It is Andrew**'s** book.

This means the book belongs to Andrew.

Whose shoe is it?

It is Tracy's shoe.

This means the shoe belongs to Tracy.

After a singular noun, we add 's

the dog's food

my brother's house

After a singular noun ending in s we can add just '

Chris' party

Paris' traffic

but usually we add 's

Chris's party

Paris's traffic

After a plural noun ending in s we add only '

his parents' car

the students' books

After a plural noun not ending in s we add 's

the children's classroom

the women's clothes

5 Complete the sentences. Write who possesses each item. The first one has been done for you.

a)   Tom's dog is big.

The _dog_____ belongs to _Tom_____.

b)   Caroline's restaurant is new.

The _____ belongs to _____.

c)   Lucy's cake is delicious.

The _____ belongs to _____.

d)   Rachel's cat is orange.

The _____ belongs to _____.

e)   Jack's car is fast.

The _____ belongs to _____.

6 Complete these sentences. Use apostrophes. The first one has been done for you.

a)   The bag belongs to Ken.

It is _Ken's bag____ .

b)   The house belongs to Robert.

It is _____ .

c)   The car belongs to Susie.

It is _____ .

d)   The money belongs to Tania.

It is _____ .

e)   The piano belongs to Jack.

It is _____ .

7 Add ☐' or ☐'s to each sentence.

a)   The dog water is cold.

b)   Chris car was slow.

c)   We visited Paris tower.

d)   Caroline coat is black.

e)   James knee is hurt.

f)   David son is young.

g)   The boss wife is friendly.

h)   I lost the teacher book.

i)   She drove to Tim house.

j)   Ross farm is large.

8 Add 〔'〕 or 〔's〕 to each sentence.

a)   The children teacher is young.

b)   These are the boys desks.

c)   The women handbags are lost.

d)   The men cars are expensive.

e)   These are the horses combs.

f)   The students computers are new.

g)   Those are the teachers offices.

h)   His parents house is large.

i)   The babies toys are on the floor.

j)   The girls dresses are dirty.

a) The cat name is Tiger.

b) Have you met Emma brothers?

c) This is Ross bag.

d) Thomas painting is in the art museum.

e) The man job is difficult.

f) My books are in my friend bag.

g) The ladies clothes are beautiful.

h) The White house is only three years old.

i) I have three dogs. The dogs meat is in the freezer.

j) Charles homework is very good.

a) Those are the teachers cars.

b) Bob shirt is green.

c) The woman baby is cute.

d) Jim swimming pool is deep.

e) These are the girls fathers.

f) Steven cushions are ripped.

g) This is my grandfather wallet.

h) The boy name is Wayne.

i) Sam is Curtis friend.